From their mami, they learned
creativity and resilience.
How to make do, make clothes last,
and make a dollar stretch.
They learned about the importance
of sharing resources.

Dedicated to all Latina visionaries and pioneers—most especially
to poderosas Melissa Gonzalez, Mia García Peña, Aida Salazar,
and Alexandra Villasante
—N.R.

I'd like to dedicate this to my parents, my number one supporters
since day one.
Para mi mamá y papá, mis seguidores número uno
desde el primer día.
—N.M.

Carolrhoda Books®
An imprint of Lerner Publishing Group, Inc.
241 First Avenue North
Minneapolis, MN 55401 USA

For reading levels and more information, look up this title at
www.lernerbooks.com.

Photographs courtesy of Joe Conzo.

Designed by Kimberly Morales.
Main body text set in Mundo Sans Std.
Typeface provided by Monotype Typography.
The illustrations in this book were created using digital media.

Library of Congress Cataloging-in-Publication Data

Names: Ramos, NoNieqa, author. | Medina, Nicole, 1995- illustrator.
Title: Best believe : the Tres Hermanas, a sisterhood for the
    common good / NoNieqa Ramos ; illustrated by Nicole Medina.
Other titles: Tres Hermanas, a sisterhood for the common good
Description: Minneapolis : Carolrhoda Books, [2024] | Includes
    bibliographical references. | Audience: Ages 6-10 years |
    Audience: Grades 2-3 | Summary: "Rhythmic verse presents
    three sisters who moved from Puerto Rico to New York City as
    children and grew up to be pioneering activists in their Bronx
    community, focusing on schools, libraries, and the arts"
    —Provided by publisher.
Identifiers: LCCN 2023021332 (print) | LCCN 2023021333 (ebook) |
    ISBN 9781728460444 (lib. bdg.) | ISBN 9781728493992 (epub)
Subjects: LCSH: Puerto Rican women—New York (State)—New
    York—Biography—Juvenile literature. | Puerto Ricans—
    New York (State)—New York—Political activity—Juvenile
    literature. | Women political activists—New York (State)—New
    York—Biography—Juvenile literature. | Sisters—New York (State)—
    New York—Biography—Juvenile literature. | Social change—New
    York (State)—New York—Juvenile literature. | Bronx (New York,
    N.Y.)—Biography. | BISAC: JUVENILE NONFICTION / Biography
    & Autobiography / Social Activists | JUVENILE NONFICTION /
    Activism & Social Justice
Classification: LCC F128.9.P85 R366 2024 (print) | LCC F128.9.P85
    (ebook) | DDC 305.48/8687295073—dc23/eng/20230602

LC record available at https://lccn.loc.gov/2023021332
LC ebook record available at https://lccn.loc.gov/2023021333

Manufactured in the United States of America
1-1009843-50383-8/16/2023

BEST BELIEVE

The Tres Hermanas,
a Sisterhood for the Common Good

written by **NoNieqa Ramos**
illustrated by **Nicole Medina**

Carolrhoda Books
Minneapolis

The Bronx is more than subways and concrete.
More than struggle.
More than the eye can see.

The Bronx is a library of stories.
Of poetry in graffiti.
Of sheroes who have changed history.

Of powerhouse families.
Of three sisters who changed destinies.
Called the Tres Hermanas by all who knew them,
Evelina Antonetty, Lillian López, and Elba Cabrera
were born and raised to lead.

EVELINA

LILLIAN

ELBA

Throughout their lives, the three sisters would earn
many a.k.a.'s, titles, and degrees.
Many call their family Bronx royalty.

EVELINA

When Evelina was a child,
she never imagined one day she'd be called a queen.

But just how do you become royalty?

Evelina and her younger sister Lillian
were born in a poor fishing village in Salinas, Puerto Rico,
on the Taíno land of Borikén.
The dos hermanas grew up in a time of widespread poverty
called the Great Depression.

From dawn to dusk, their single mami hustled.
But pobrecita, she always struggled.

How could she make sure her niñas
had a life where they didn't work dawn to dusk?
Mami's heart ached,
but she made an important decision.
Evelina would leave Borikén
and move in with her Tía Vicenta and Tío Godreau
in Nueva York in Spanish Harlem.

Mami went into labor with her third baby
the night before Evelina's journey.

Cradling Elba in her sleep,
Evelina wept
for all the moments she'd be missing.

So how did Evelina
become a woman who
would write herstory?

Evelina didn't have a lot of money.
But you best believe,
she had something more precious—
valentía, bravery.

On a bright morning, Evelina said goodbye.
The family hugged. They prayed. They cried.

From the deck of a steamship,
Evelina waved,
dreaming of what lay ahead.
Would she like her new home?
Her new school?
Would she make friends?

Though the American Dream was supposed to
be a golden door to opportunity,
young Evelina would witness Puerto Ricans' harsh reality.

Contrary to the promise of life, liberty, and
the pursuit of happiness,
they experienced discrimination because of
their skin color, their heritage, and their language.
Was the United States a land of broken promises?

Evelina was furious. But what were her first action steps?
Her Tía Vicenta showed her how anger can be a gift.
Because it meant her eyes were open to injustice.
Because it meant she had the imagination to do
something about it.

Tía showed Evelina how to
problem-solve and
organize with her barrio.
Evelina met Puerto Rican
activist Jesús Colón.
He spoke with her about
how workers deserve dignity,
how serving the people is
everybody's responsibility.

From her elders,
Evelina learned to fight.
Not with fists, but with her
power to unite.

EVELINA & TÍA VICENTA

JESÚS COLÓN & EVELINA

Two years after Evelina's journey,
she was joined in Harlem
by Lillian, Elba, and Mami!

Life at the Godreau residence was never lonely.
After work, Tío would bring home treats, jokes, and stories.
Elba loved him so much she called him Papi.

And when Tío Godreau wasn't cooking up a storm in the kitchen,
he was hustling to promote dancers, singers, and musicians.

Imagine the sala galas at the apartamento de Tío Godreau!
Songsters Bobby Capó and Machito singing Elba ¡Feliz cumpleaños!
The whole barrio surrounding her as she blew out the candles
over a triple-layer bizcocho.

Or singer Mario Bauza
crooning a Cuban lullaby.
Each hermana smiling
as sleep tugged on their eyes.

What were their dreams
as they drifted to sleep?
What were the dreams of little girls
who would become Bronx royalty?

You best believe no one was gonna tell Evelina
what to do or who to be.

She thought about how kids at school
made fun of her accent
and how they laughed at anyone
who didn't speak English—yet.

Evelina was ready to help at the young age of thirteen.
She used her new ability
to speak English and Spanish
to help newcomers to the community.

She helped them read contracts and
bills written in English.
Helped them talk to landlords about
fixing problems in their apartments.

She protested when neighbors who couldn't afford rent were evicted,
their belongings tossed onto the street.
She traveled on a trolley to bring her neighbors groceries.

Imagine how busy Evelina was with helping others,
school, and family responsibilities!

You best believe,
the Tres Hermanas had learned neighbors were family.
That taking care of one another in times of need
is the superpower of community.

Evelina grew up, married,
and moved to the South Bronx in the 1940s.
As a parent with three children in school,
she saw disparity.
How white children were treated well,
while Black and brown children were still treated badly.
Teachers gave children who read and spoke only Spanish
lessons and tests in English.
When children failed, they said there was no point
in teaching Puerto Rican kids to read,
they'd never succeed.

Evelina was furious.
Again, her anger was a gift.

Evelina said, "I began to see the school as an island.
At three o'clock, the school officials closed the doors and left the community. . . .

There were no teachers in the school from our community."
She fought back against the school system by raising an army of mamis.

In 1965, Evelina created the United Bronx Parents, UBP, to empower.
She said, "It is up to us as parents to demand and get the school authorities,
the legislators and city officials to give our children the education
which is rightfully ours. Our children can become the educators, doctors
and leaders of tomorrow. Don't let anyone tell us differently."

Sometimes people said Evelina was too loud.
They called her mean names.
Hoped she'd have a seat. Be still. Pipe down.
But Evelina was defiant. Proud.
And her youngest hermana, Elba, helped her hold it down.

Elba was her secretary, her support, her MVP.
Together, they demanded schools hire
quality principals and teachers of color
and pay them a good salary.
They advocated for bilingual education.
For students to have healthy school meals and
clean and safe spaces for learning.

ELBA

And since "hunger doesn't take a vacation,"
Elba became the office manager and program director
for their summer feeding program for the whole city.

You best believe in the sacred bond of siblings.
The magic of hermanas working together
to build a dream.

In 1968, while studying for her degree,
Elba helped Evelina found Hostos Community College,
which filled an important community need.
They were a team.
Hostos would provide an affordable education
that honored Black and brown cultural roots and contributions to society.

And in 1976, the hermanas defended it
when Mayor Abraham Beame tried to close it down permanently.
For nine days, Evelina, faculty, students, Vietnam vets, and artists
occupied the Hostos Community College administrative building.

Despite arrests of forty protesters,
they achieved victory!
The protesters' actions kept the college open,
and today it is considered one of the best community colleges in New York City.

What about middle sister, Lillian?
She was considered quiet.
Reserved. Introverted. Discreet.
But you best believe,
her contributions were just as important to herstory.

Despite the challenges of being a Puerto Rican woman
facing sexism and bigotry,
Lillian earned a library science degree from Columbia University.
She would become the South Bronx project director in charge of nine libraries!

In time, she became the first Puerto Rican administrator
in her role as Bronx borough coordinator
in charge of ALL Bronx libraries!

Imagine books as magical portals.
But back in the 1960s, only English-speaking readers had keys.
Lillian fought to introduce Spanish and bilingual books
and hire Spanish-speaking staff
in Bronx and Manhattan libraries.

Matter of fact, in 1975
when Mayor Beame tried to save money for the city
by targeting ONLY libraries
in Black, brown, and poor communities—
not libraries in white communities—
Lillian *was* the key.

By closing these libraries,
the mayor was robbing families.
Taking away the power of reading to create opportunity.
To empower people to imagine and create their own destinies.

The Tres Hermanas and UBP fought back against Mayor Beame.
They took over the Hunts Point and Tremont Libraries
with the help of Lillian—who had quietly slipped them the keys.
They moved in and locked them down in protest for two weeks.

The mayor got the message and figured out better ways to save the city money.
Imagine the Tres Hermanas' victory party!

But even with victory, you best believe
the Tres Hermanas
had to remind one another to pause.
To breathe.
To sleep.
To eat.

To play.
To laugh hard.
To pray.
That changing the world doesn't happen in a day.

In 1978, the hermanas celebrated another victory.
Elba graduated with a bachelor of arts degree.
She became a director at the Association of Hispanic Arts
and had a TV show interviewing famous Latino stars!

Then she became marketing director at the Lehman Center for the Performing Arts,
which brought music, dance, and theater from around the world—
at affordable prices—to the people of the Bronx.

Elba later hosted a weekly radio show spotlighting Hispanic excellence.
She was a lifelong arts, culture, and community advocate,
organizing and promoting artists who became queridos amigos, dear friends.
Many call her La Madrina de las Artes!

The Tres Hermanas believed in themselves.
The Tres Hermanas believed in one another.
You best believe the Tres Hermanas believed in you.
Do you believe in you too?
They believed in your talents.
They believed in your gifts.
They believed in your intelligence.
They believed you deserve happiness.

They believed you deserve
safe housing and healthy food.
Great teachers.
A top-notch school.
Books and libraries.
They believed what you deserve has nothing to do
with having a lot of money.

So are the Tres Hermanas really royalty?

As an adult, Evelina was told she was a queen. She replied, "I don't answer to being a queen. I answer to being a good human being."

"We will never stop struggling here in the Bronx, even though they've destroyed it around us. We would pitch tents if we have to rather than move from here. We would fight back. There is nothing we would not do. They will never take us away from here. I am very much a part of this and I am going to leave. And... children...

AUTHOR'S NOTE

In the Bronx, on the southeast corner of East 156th Street and Prospect Avenue, you can find Dra. Evelina Antonetty Way. That sign is a marker of the borough's rich history of Puerto Rican migrants, including the three sisters who became known as Las Tres Hermanas del Bronx. But when I grew up there, the Bronx had a reputation—still does—and it wasn't for having a rich history. Movies and television depicted it as a crime-infested dump. If I told people I came from the Bronx, I got asked if the Bronx had trees. (It does. Parks full of trees and flowers and big rocks to climb and places to jump rope. And an entire Bronx Zoo and Botanical Gardens. Oh, and schools like my high school—Cardinal Spellman—from which Supreme Court judge and Boricua Sonia Sotomayor graduated. I digress.) The Bronx was and still is the poorest borough in New York City. The struggle is real in the Boogie Down, but it's far from all that defines the borough.

The Bronx's wealth comes from its people, its families, its activists, educators, artists, librarians, and more. It comes from all the many people who make it a place I keep coming back to—both in my visits to the New York Public Library of the Bronx and in books like this one. Sometimes an inheritance is more than money. Think about all we have inherited from Eva, Evelina, Elba, and Lillian!

I will forever be grateful to Bronx photojournalist Joe Conzo Jr. for connecting me to his Titi Elba and for his incredible generosity in sharing a treasure trove of historical photos. Tremendous love to querida Elba, ever the poderosa, who took the time to educate me on the remarkable history of her life and the Bronx.

The fight for justice and equality continues. Part of the battle is won by honoring sheroes like the Tres Hermanas, Evelina, Lillian, and Elba, and following their courageous examples.

Scan the QR code for further resources and additional information about the Tres Hermanas.

qrs.lernerbooks.com/best-believe

SOURCE NOTES

"I began to . . . from our community" Laura Kaplan, "United Bronx Parents and the Struggle for Educational Equality in the 1960s," *Theory, Research, and Action in Urban Education* 4, no. 2, spring 2016, https://traue.commons.gc.cuny.edu/volume-iv-issue-2-spring-2016/1050-2.

"It is up to . . . tell us differently" Lana Dee Povitz, "Hunger Doesn't Take a Vacation: The Food Activism of United Bronx Parents," in *Women's Activism and "Second Wave" Feminism*, eds. Barbara Molony and Jennifer Nelson (New York: Bloomsbury Academic, 2017), https://www.bloomsburycollections.com/book/womens-activism-and-second-wave-feminism/ch1-hunger-doesn-t-take-a-vacation-the-food-activism-of-united-bronx-parents.

"hunger doesn't take a vacation" Povitz.

"I don't answer . . . good human being" Elba Cabrera, interview with the author, November 30, 2021.

"We will never stop . . . going to leave" Saleema Walter, "Evelina López Antonetty: The Mother of the Bronx," Muslim Public Affairs Council, March 30, 2023, https://www.mpac.org/article/evelina-lopez-antonetty-the-mother-of-the-bronx.

"The desperation there . . . on a boat" "Remembering a Neighborhood Activist," *Mott Haven (NY) Herald*, August 2, 2011, https://motthavenherald.com/2011/08/02/remembering-a-neighborhood-activist.

"My role is . . . the everyday person" "Lillian López Papers," Archives of the Puerto Rican Diaspora, Centro Center for Puerto Rican Studies, accessed July 25, 2023, https://centroarchives.hunter.cuny.edu/repositories/2/resources/26.

"If there was . . . from my community" Miss Rosen, "A New York Exhibition Remembers 'The Hell Lady of the Bronx,'" *i-D*, September 14, 2022, https://i-d.vice.com/en/article/epza4j/dr-evelina-lopez-antonetty-100-centennial-exhibition-new-york.

"The goal of . . . and the community" "Lillian López Papers."

"We will be delighted . . . to the problems" Povitz.

"She was the spirit . . . and her organizing" "Remembering a Neighborhood Activist."

"We were all born . . . hunger, and determination." Rosen.

BE IN THE KNOW

administrator: someone who makes important decisions and solves problems. As a Puerto Rican administrator, Lillian made decisions that helped underserved and neglected communities.

a.k.a.: an abbreviation meaning "also known as." Another a.k.a. for Evelina was Titi, which is an affectionate name for a tía or aunt.

barrio: Spanish word for neighborhood

bigotry: racism

bilingual: a person speaks two languages

bizcocho: a word that means "cake" in Spanish; spoken in certain places, including Puerto Rico

Borikén: the name for Puerto Rico in the Taíno language. Taínos are the largest group of Indigenous or Native people living in the Caribbean islands. They live in the islands that are now Puerto Rico, Dominican Republic, Haiti, Cuba, and the Bahamas.

borough: one of the five divisions of New York City

the Bronx: a borough of New York City, New York; nicknamed the Boogie Down Bronx in honor of its history as the birthplace of rap and hip-hop music

Bobby Capó: singer and songwriter Félix Manuel "Bobby" Rodríguez Capó; wrote and sang the beloved song "Soñando con Puerto Rico" (Dreaming of Puerto Rico)

Jesús Colón: an activist and community organizer who wrote poetry and stories about his experiences as an Afro-Puerto Rican living in New York

dignity: the right of a person to be valued and respected because they are a human being

discrimination: unfair treatment because of age, disability, gender, gender identity, religion or beliefs, birthplace, race, skin color, or sexuality

disparity: a noticeable and often unfair difference

East Harlem: a neighborhood in the New York borough of Manhattan; birthplace of Latin jazz

economy: consists of all people who make things, all people who use things, and all buying and selling of those things

evict: when a landlord forces a tenant (renter) to leave a property for nonpayment of rent or other reasons

feliz cumpleaños: happy birthday in Spanish

hermanas: sisters in Spanish

injustice: unfairness

landlord: a businessperson or company that owns buildings or land and earns money by charging rent to people (tenants) who want to use them

Latino: a term used most often in the United States to describe a person of Latin American origin or descent

legislators: elected officials responsible for making laws within a city, state, or country

Machito: a renowned musician; with Mario Bauzá, created the first Afro-Cuban jazz recording

marketing: telling people what your company makes and helping them understand why they would want or need it

national flower of Puerto Rico: the Flor de Maga; looks very similar to the amapola. The national flower is depicted on the cover of this book. The flowers in the book's interior are amapolas, in honor of Evelina's favorite flower.

niñas: Spanish for "girls"

Nueva York: Spanish for New York

pobrecita: Spanish for "poor thing"

sexism: unfair treatment because of gender; often directed toward girls and women

Taíno: Indigenous people of the Caribbean

United Bronx Parents (UBP): an organization founded by Evelina Antonetty in 1965 that united Puerto Rican and African American parents and activists concerned with the quality of their South Bronx public schools

TIMELINE

1920s: Puerto Rican activist Evangelina (Eva) Cruz López believes Puerto Rico should be free from the control of the United States.

1922: Eva gives birth to Evelina López.

1925: Eva gives birth to Lillian López.

1928: Hurricane San Felipe Segundo flattens sugar factories and wipes out Puerto Rico's coffee crop, destroying the island's economy. Thousands of people are left homeless.

1929: The Great Depression begins. In the ten years that follow, it devastates the global economy. Millions of people lose their jobs and homes.

1933: Eva gives birth to Elba Cabrera. She sends eleven-year-old Evelina on a five-day journey by steamship to live with her Tía Vicenta and Tío Godreau in New York.

> "The desperation there must have been, to send your child alone on a boat . . ."
>
> —Anita Antonetty, Evelina's granddaughter

Eva Cruz (*right*) with her daughters: Evelina (*center top*), Lillian (*left*), and Elba (*center bottom*)

1935: Eva, Lillian, and Elba journey to New York City and reunite with Evelina in East Harlem.

Late 1930s: Teenaged Evelina and her Tía Vicenta work with community leaders such as Jesús Colón to fight for workers' rights. Evelina helps neighbors who aren't fluent in English.

1940: Evelina marries at eighteen years old.

Early 1940s: Evelina moves to the South Bronx. As one of the first Latinas hired by the United Auto Workers, a US labor union, she helps prepare Spanish-speaking people for the workforce.

1944: Lillian graduates from Washington Irving High School.

1947: Evelina divorces her first husband.

1951: Elba graduates from Bronx Vocational High School with training in secretarial work and bookkeeping.

1952: Lillian enrolls at Hunter College.

1955: Evelina marries Donald Antonetty. Her mother and sisters move to the South Bronx to live near her. Neighbors stop by regularly for help and advice.

1959: Lillian graduates from Hunter College with a bachelor's degree.

1960–1962: Lillian earns a masters of library science degree from Columbia University and advocates for better library services for New York City's Spanish-speaking residents.

> "[My role is to get the library to] come down to earth and serve the needs of the every day person."
>
> —Lillian López

1962: When her daughter Anita starts school, Evelina becomes president of PS 5's Parent Teacher Association. She spearheads the first Head Start program in New York City, which supports children from birth to the age of five.

1964: Evelina founds the United Friends and Neighbors of the Bronx at 645 Union Avenue to help parents and families have a voice in their school community.

1965: United Friends and Neighbors of the Bronx becomes United Bronx Parents. UBP supports parents in the fight for hiring educators who look and sound like their students, accurate representation of Puerto Rican and African American history in the classroom, a fair disciplinary system that doesn't target BIPOC students, clean and safe school buildings, and healthy school food. In the community, they fight for tenant rights, fair housing, voting rights, the removal of garbage and toxic waste dumped in Black and brown neighborhoods, and more.

> "If there was an issue, [Evelina] was on the frontlines letting it be known: 'You're not closing down this school or this fire department. You're not going to take this away from my community.'"
>
> —Evelina's grandson, photojournalist Joe Conzo Jr.

1966–1978: Elba works with United Bronx Parents as a secretary, office manager, and director for their summer feeding program.

1967: Lillian spearheads the South Bronx Project (SBP), which brings bilingual story times to schools, churches, and playgrounds. She hires trailblazing Puerto Rican librarian Pura Belpré (who had retired) to teach the staff how to create puppets, costumes, and props for story times.

> "The goal of the project was to break down barriers between the library and the community."
>
> —Lillian López

Evelina at the headquarters of United Bronx Parents

1969: Evelina, Elba, and UBP fight to improve conditions for children of color in school cafeterias. UBP invites elected officials for a lunch meeting. The menu contains items that students are typically served, including stale bread and sour macaroni. An assemblyman gets sick. UBP then hosts another school lunch and serves officials nourishing foods—sweet potatoes, ham hocks, and plantains—that cost a fraction of what the city spends on school lunches.

> **"We will be delighted to serve you a 'real school lunch' the way it should be. We expect you, our elected representatives, to . . . tell us what you have done to achieve our demands. We are not interested in being told <u>why</u> these problems exist. We want <u>solutions</u> to the problems!"**
>
> —United Bronx Parents

1970: To draw attention to the ongoing problem of waste in the school lunch program caused by poor-quality food, UBP dumps full plastic garbage bags of food collected from school trash bins at a government building in downtown Manhattan.

Evelina helps transform Elba's former elementary school, PS 25, into the first public school in the US to offer classes in both English and Spanish. Other schools soon follow.

> **"She was the spirit and the force behind bilingual education in the United States, to put it simply. It would not have happened in the quick form and fashion that it did if it were not for her energy and her organizing."**
>
> —Vicky Gholson, a former United Bronx Parents board member

Evelina receives an honorary doctorate from Manhattan College.

> **"We were all born with PhDs—degrees in poverty, hunger, and determination."**
>
> —Evelina Antonetty

1970s: Lillian joins the American Library Association and the New York Library Association.

1971: Evelina, Elba, and UBP run a free summer meals program for 150,000 New York City children.

1972: Lillian is put in charge of the Special Services Office of the New York Public Library, which allows her to do projects similar to the SBP all across New York City.

1973–1978: Evelina, Elba, and UBP save Hostos Community College from closing down.

1978: Elba graduates from SUNY at Old Westbury with honors. She begins working at the Association of Hispanic Arts, where she promotes the activities of more than one hundred arts organizations, creates the Directory of Hispanic Arts Organizations, and hosts a weekly television show.

1978–1988: Elba becomes the marketing director at the Lehman Center for the Performing Arts.

1979: Lillian becomes the Bronx Borough coordinator, responsible for thirty-three branch libraries.

1980–1982: Lillian is appointed to the National Commission on Libraries and Information Sciences' Minorities Task Force.

1984: Evelina Antonetty transitions to the afterlife. Her daughter Lorraine Montenegro becomes the director of UBP.

1985: Lillian retires after twenty-five years of library service.

1988–1991: Elba is the director of Hispanic Affairs/Admissions at the Center for the Media Arts.

1992–2002: Elba works with Girl Scouts of the USA.

2003: Elba officially retires, though she stays active on several boards, including the Hostos Community College Foundation. She receives numerous honors, including the Network of Bronx Women Laureate Award and the Latino Plus 50 Lifetime Achievement Award.

2005: Lillian López transitions to the afterlife.

2022: Centro, Hunter College, Hostos Community College, and the Evelina Centennial Committee celebrate the life and legacy of Evelina Antonetty in a weeklong event that includes voter registration drives, tree plantings, and art and educational exhibitions.

**The Tres Hermanas (*left to right*):
Evelina, Elba, and Lillian**

SELECTED BIBLIOGRAPHY

"A Celebration of the Life and Times of Evelina Antonetty." Evelina 100, October 4, 2022. https://www.evelina100.digital/.

Elba Cabrera Papers, Archives of the Puerto Rican Diaspora. Center for Puerto Rican Studies, Hunter College, CUNY. Accessed March 31, 2023. https://centroarchives.hunter .cuny.edu/repositories/2/resources/35.

"Evelina Lives: A Short Documentary." YouTube video, 9:22. Posted by BronxNet, September 2022. https://www.youtube.com/watch?v=U2P-JLodckU&t=8s.

Flores-Hostos, Aurora. "'I'm a Mother, and I'm a Mother': A Eulogy for Evelina, the Hell Lady of the Bronx." The Latinx Project, September 16, 2022. https://www.latinxproject .nyu.edu/intervenxions/1wyt8fmrwrsdsyf3z745mjpjzl549p.

"OPEN BxRx Friday | Evelina Antonetty Centennial Celebration: Fort Apache the Bronx Viewing & Panel." Bronxnet video, 16:06, September 2, 2022. https://www.bronxnet.org /watch/videos/15774/.

Povitz, Lana Dee. "Hunger Doesn't Take a Vacation: The Food Activism of United Bronx Parents." In *Women's Activism and "Second Wave" Feminism*, edited by Barbara Molony and Jennifer Nelson. London: Bloomsbury Academic, 2017, 15–36. https://www .bloomsburycollections.com/book/womens-activism-and-second-wave-feminism /ch1-hunger-doesn-t-take-a-vacation-the-food-activism-of-united-bronx-parents.

SUGGESTED FURTHER READING

Aldamuy Denise, Anika. *Planting Stories: The Life of Librarian and Storyteller Pura Belpré*. New York: Harper, 2019.

González, Karina Nicole. *The Coquíes Still Sing*. New York: Roaring Brook, 2022.

Hill, Laban Carrick. *When the Beat Was Born: DJ Kool Herc and the Creation of Hip Hop*. New York: Roaring Brook, 2013.

Hoang, Zara González. *A New Kind of Wild*. New York: Dial, 2020.

Orenstein-Cardona, Anna. *The Tree of Hope: The Miraculous Rescue of Puerto Rico's Beloved Banyan*. Minneapolis: Beaming Books, 2022.

Sotomayor, Sonia. *Turning Pages: My Life Story*. New York: Philomel, 2018.